A Photo Handbook of Weeds Identification and Green Grass Lawn Care for Picture Perfect Turf

NC Weed Killer

DEDICATION

This book is for all those weekend warriors
who really just want a beautiful lawn to enjoy- not to fight with.

ACKNOWLEDGMENTS

I want to thank all of the creative people who went before me,

solving problems, finding new ways,

and always feeling the driving need to share knowledge and insight.

CONTENTS

NOTE FROM A TRANSPLANT

As I mentioned earlier, I felt the need for this book when I moved from St. Louis, MO to Raleigh, NC. I have always gardened and tended lawns (I've reclaimed quite a few!), but the shift in growing zone made me painfully aware of what I did not know. A good simple place to start would have been welcome, so now I'm going to leave this for those who follow, and for those who are staying put but starting on a lawn care mission. I hope the pictures that follow with help you your own game of "Is it weed? or, is it wonderful?!"

For those of you moving from colder climes, let me suggest that one of the biggest things you will need to learn is a mental shift from the short growing season North to the more southerly view. In the North, the idea was to nurture and value every little thing that sprouted and turned green. From 7c to the South, you can pretty much assume that if it is a native plant and it falls on the ground, it will grow. Those little lantanas that were coaxed to 12" in St. Louis and then killed over winter are perennials in Raleigh, and almost invasive.

The attitude shift? As much as it may pain you, be ready to cut back, kill out and spend a lot of time controlling what you spent three months coddling through a short life up North. Cases in point: do some research on kudzu, the plant that is eating the South, and, after June 15th , try to find a highway sign in Raleigh that isn't hidden in the brush and trees.

This concept will come into play when I discuss nuking some of the more offensive weeds. In some areas it is easier to get the good stuff to grow than it is to get the bad stuff to stop growing.

SOME BASICS

In order for good stuff to grow you need the right seed for the good stuff, and you need the right growing conditions. I will deal with reseeding later on, but too often the condition of the soil is over-looked. Between testing for pH and doing a little top-dressing, the soil condition can be controlled.

Most grass is looking for a neutral 6.5 – 7.0 pH to grow well. Most weeds are looking for an acidic 5.0 – 6.0 soil condition. If we can make the soil a more neutral pH, then our battle for grass and against weeds is starting on our terms.

There are soil test kits on the market, though I have to admit my main take-away there is a feeling of incompetence.

Some gardening groups, Master Gardener associations and state or local extension services will perform the tests for you, or at least point you in the right direction. Even some cost here could bring big results.

If you need to sweeten the soil, lime is relatively inexpensive and a drop spreader makes quick work of it.

Depending on your soil, there are a number of paths to take for correction. Between sand, compost, composted mulch, or just leaving well-enough alone, the correct option needs to be determined by you, either through some research or by using the advice of local experts. The one caution I know I can make is this- if you decide to add mulch or compost, be very careful with pH! The composting process creates a great deal of acid. You will need to compensate for this or you will be creating a rich environment that kills grass and encourages weeds!

THE TACTICS

The backbone of my strategy is to use feed or weed-and-feed four times per year, with the additional application of a pre-emergent 2 – 3 times per year. This will maintain a ready supply of growing nutrients, allow a killing of generic weeds as needed, and prevent the bad stuff from germinating so you won't have to worry about identifying it or killing it.

Most bigger name lawn care supplement companies have seasonal plans for feeding and weed control which you can follow. To the North, you can count on a better over-winter weed kill and a shorter growing season to control. Towards zone 9, you are looking at more of a 12-month growing and control calendar. In Raleigh, I am somewhat in the middle, as are a lot of us, so I will expand a little on my schedule and logic so you can adapt it to your own environment.

In Raleigh (7c) my main problems come from annual bluegrass (annual poa) and from stilt grass. The annual poa likes to germinate close to the same time as my preferred fescue. The stilt grass germinates in the Spring, but before the crabgrass. In addition, it is a true grass, so there is no selective herbicide that will kill it without killing the rest of the lawn. Plus, too much nitrogen in June-July-August and the brown spot fungus throws a party. My strategy?

Basically, I target my Fall reseeding and work around that.

I want to reseed my fescue in October when the temperatures run 60 – 80 degrees. That means I want the effect or any pre-emergent dissipated, so the fescue seed will germinate and grow. As a normal application of pre-emergent (generic) lasts about three months and I know I want the October to December months to be pre-emergent free I want to apply pre-emergent in Jan/Feb, April and Jul. (See the table below.)

	Pre-emergent	Reseed	Weed & Feed	Special Notes
Oct – Dec	NO	YES, early October	Fall Feeding	Spray Image for poa after new fescue is strong
Feb –	yes – stilt grass	no	Early Spring Feed	Spot control
Apr –	yes – crab grass	no	Late Spring Weed & Feed	Spot control
Jul –	yes – all weeds	no	Summer Conditioner Feed	Spot control

My Fall feeding will be in November to avoid harming the new fescue. This is when I will also spray with Image® Weed Control because I have found it very effective against the annual poa.

January through March can be wintry here (you may need to wait a day for a snow fall to melt before you golf again…) and the temperatures generally are low enough to curtail most plant growth. But the stilt grass can start germinating in March, so I want the pre-emergent down sometime in February at the latest. February, early March, is a good time for fertilizer as well.

April through June is when then cards are shown. If you miss-guessed, or missed, a pre-emergent and weed kill, you will start to see stilt grass and crab grass. If you don't see them, you did it correctly. You win!

Get the Late Spring feed down in early April or there will be too much nitrogen in June.

That is my general plan. You need to adjust for your growing zone and grass type conditions, but this should give you the foundation ideas.

Set a time table based on set goals, like reseeding in October. Work around that, and you will be on your way.

Some tips that may help your planning:

- All seeds have their own particular temperature ranges for germinating. Research your grass type and your local temperature ranges to plan out grass reseeding and weed prevention.
- Most trees and plants will start active growth once the ground temperature rises above 50 degrees. This is dependent on the temperature at the depth of the plant roots.
- Forsythia have shallow roots, so when you see the forsythia flower, you had better have applied your pre-emergent and first weed preventions. Forsythia lives where the grass and weeds l;ive.

- Brown spot in lawns is a fungus that will start if turf conditions are humid and if the temperature, including overnight, runs over 70 degrees for three days or more. If you have any doubts, spread a lawn fungicide before that temperature run. Once brown spot starts, it is difficult to recover from unscathed.

This might be a good time to mention that in the weeds photographs that follow, I do not have a picture of the annual poa. Basically, it looks like bright green healthy wonderful grass. You can find pictures on any university ag web site. What I do have is a picture of the lawn after the "beautiful grass" of May has burnt out in June, leaving ugly bare dirt with only islands of fescue. This is why I worked so hard with the trial and error to develop this plan!

I should also mention that most pre-emergent products don't actually stop the seed from germinating; they kill off the tender first shoot growth from the seed. Keep this in mind when transplanting into treated areas, or when getting pre-emergent into flower beds. I generally use pre-emergent on my flower beds and then start self-seeding flowers separately from seed I collected in the Fall. Them I wait to transplant until the young plants have at least 'teen-age' roots. This way I keep the weeds out of the flowers and I can keep track of what is growing where. But my flower garden strategies are for another book…

These two steps alone, the use of a four step annual feed (and weed) plus extra pre-emergent as required, will probably solve 80% of your lawn care problems.

SPOT TREATING WITH SELECTIVE HERBACIDES

Generally, using the spreader to apply pre-emergent, feed, and weed & feed will get most of the weeds that have been creating problems plus you will be adding the nutrients for a healthy turf. But there is always that missed spot, the visiting bird or animal, and the wind to bring weed seed into the yard. Now it is time to start working on that final 20% of the problem.

The next tactic is to find a good spot weed controller that you can spray in targeted areas. You want to be able to mix up a one-to-two gallon tank. Rather than doing a blanket broadcast spraying all over the place, you want to be able to spray on weeds as you find them or in areas that you think might be potential beginnings of weeds. This way you will stop the weeds before they mature and set seed.

The first phase of this spot spraying is to use a selective weed killer that will kill weeds but not the lawn. There are several good products on the market, and in my transition between growing zones, I found that some are better in certain zones. This book isn't intended as a commercial, so I will leave it to you and your local lawn care store to select the product that works best for your particular problem.

Of course, the primary intent of this book is to help you focus on what you need to do the get the best lawn with the least effort, which means efficient use of your time and dollars.

And that is the reason for the pictures of weeds. If you can identify the weeds you need to eliminate, then you can find the best targeted weed killer. Any quality weed killer will have the targeted weeds listed on the packaging, so you will be able to select the correct product.

One glitch you may run into is that any plant will go by a variety of names, so you may want to do a little research on the web to discover other names, if you don't find your default name right off. An example of this came about when I spent some time in southern Missouri. Talking about flowers, the locals kept mentioning that the 'flags' would be coming soon, that someone always had the prettiest 'flags', that someone else's were beautiful this year. Expecting to see something unusual, I couldn't find what they were talking about. So I asked. It turns out that 'flags' was the local vernacular for irises, which I had seen but overlooked, sure of the name I knew them by.

One big point to be made with any of the chemical treatments I have been discussing centers on manufacturing instructions.

Read the packaging and follow the directions. Any chemicals being added to the environment run completely counter to the logic of "more is better"! Use as directed, and just like any prescription you take, consider interaction and build up. No matter how targeted, any weed killer is going to stress the good stuff some, and a lot of 'stress' can lead to problems. Just as applied fertilizer will also feed the weeds, so applied fertilizer will apply some stress to the grass. Go lightly. If you don't see the expected results in two weeks, go lightly again. If you go too heavy-handed, you may be looking forward to reseeding sooner than scheduled!

And while we are talking about heavy-handed, watch you aim, as well! Most flowers and decorative shrubbery can be more sensitive to weed killers than the weeds are. Watch out for spraying the wrong thing, and watch out for "drift", where just a light breeze can carry the spray onto the delicate flowers. It is easy to fall into a pattern of finding weeds in your peripheral vision and working a continuous spray, but sometimes your peripheral vision doesn't have the detail you need. Like most things you shoot (guns, arrows, your mouth) it can be impossible to take it back. I have seen too many edge-of-the-lawn hosta corpses that have served as testimony to this.

Along this vein, I will say that I am not a proponent of hose end spraying of weed control. Unless you have a huge lawn with no flower or shrub borders (and no neighbors with flower or shrub borders!) the lack of control of a hose spray can be asking for trouble. I am a big proponent of constructive exercise. Mix up a tank of weed control and spray with a wand. Walk around a lot. You and the yard will be better off for it. (And keep these overspray and drift concerns in mind when thinking about using a rotary spreader.)

One brand of selective weed killer that I will identify in this book is Image® Herbicide. It targets quite a few common weeds, but I have found it especially effective against Annual Bluegrass (Annual Poa), which I consider one of my two main enemies. (Stilt grass is my other nemesis, and that will be addressed in the next section.) If annual poa is one of your problems, Image® Herbicide needs to be in your arsenal.

SPOT TREATING WITH NON-SELECTIVE HERBACIDES

There are times when finesse is useless and inefficient. Sometimes a scorched earth policy can be the beginning of a brighter future. The "weed <u>AND</u> grass killer" solutions comes into play.

For me, there are four situations which call for this tactic:

1. Stiltgrass – that has been missed, or evaded the pre-emergent treatment
2. Poison Ivy - always
3. Annual Bluegrass - if it doesn't respond to a selective (may be too mature) and pre-emergent
4. Dallis grass – which can be as stubborn as it can be (initially!) localized into clumps

There are several different types of these non-selective herbicides on the market; I'll leave the choice to you and your lawn care vendor. But there are a few comments that should be made.

They are called non-selective for a reason. If they are sprayed onto a plant, it will die. I have not seen it effect tree trunks, but if it touches green, the green will turn brown. "Sorry!" is not an antidote. FOLLOW MANUFACTURERS DIRECTIONS. These products are made with the safety of people, pets and other furry things in mind, but you are talking about killing stuff. Keep the guns, arrows and mouths in mind.

Poison Ivy may not often be found in your yard, but I have found it all over, spread by seed- or some means. You can try pulling it out of beds and lawns, but the roots may be an issue. Nuke it.

The Stiltgrass that has evaded the pre-emergent must be dealt with either mechanically (pulling by hand) or with a

1. Mow tall
2. Mow light
3. Mow often

Mow Tall

There is a crisp cleanness to be found in a power mowed lawn the day it has been mowed! The fresh smell, the new green, the even smooth finish. But-

Mowing too short has several problems that can become the foundation for a troublesome season ahead. Too short and too much moisture escapes. Too short and you are cutting below the leaf of the grass blade and you damage the crown which is growing that blade. And if you don't actually cut the crown, you can still leave it too exposed to the sun, so it burns and grows nothing.

As well, cut the grass too short and you expose the soil to sun so that weed seed blown or carried into your yard has a well-nourished, moist enough, cuddly little place to germinate and grow.

Cut you lawn as high as recommended (like 2 ½ inches for fescue) and you will have better moisture control, undamaged grass growing plants, and no place for weed seed to get the light it needs to germinate and develop.

Unless your intention is to kill it, your lawn is going to grow at the rate that the weather dictates. Cutting it short is not going to save you any mowing sessions over the course of the season.

Mow Light

There are plenty of you reading this book who have circumstances that demand using a power mower, probably a rotary and maybe a riding mower. Maybe you need the power assist to cover a large or hilly yard. But there is another way that you should think about.

I have used a power assisted rotary mower for years. My yard was usually too soft (top soil laid over clay) to use a riding mower without cutting ruts all over. But then I decided to try another option that may appeal to you.

The current offerings in hand push reel mowers is completely different from the heavy, clunky, impossible to push versions of the past. Those may now qualify as child abuse. The current offerings allow good height adjustment, are light, and the cutting reels are easy to adjust so they cut clean without much resistance.

Some of the big pluses for these machines:

- they are lighter than any power mower so they can be used at any time without damaging the grass or the turf.
- being lighter, they are easier to maneuver, so it is easier to cut the lawn in a variety of patterns to avoid the ruts made by heavier wheels.
- they give the grass blade a scissor-type cut, rather than a high-speed tear, which guards against water loss and damaged plant tissue open to disease.
- once the grass height is reached, regular mowing will look as even and polished as a rotary job.

Mow Often

Being a proponent of constructive exercise, these people-powered reel mowers are light enough so you could mow the yard, or parts of it, every day without stressing the yard while earning yourself lots of exercise steps. Beats walking in aimless circles around the neighborhood. (I think…)

The frequent mowing will help the most grass possible grow up, rather than stay laying down matted, and any weeds that do start to grow will get clipped before they get a root-hold and will naturally die off.

That said, I do also use my power rotary on occasion. Sometimes my schedule or a stretch of grass-perfect weather has the grass growing taller than the reel mower can handle well, so I'll power cut it. But I do have the power mower set to cut about ½ inch taller than the reel mower, so I can get back onto the reel schedule right away.

The other reason I use the power mower is to mulch up the leaves and small twigs that build up, falling from my very wooded area. I rarely use the power mower more than once per month once my early Spring catch-up mulching is done.

The cost of a reel mower purchase is minimal compared to a power mower, and there isn't much to repair. For the quality of cut and the opportunity for bearable, rewarding exercise, the reel mower might make a perfect second machine.

A Few Tools

While I'm on the subject of real work, I want to quickly mention three tools I find invaluable for lawn care.

The first is a loop hoe, pictured above. Unlike the usual hacking type hoe, the finer looped blade of this hoe will cut weeds off right at the ground line, setting back their growth substantially. A couple of trims like this and they give up. The hoe is not intended for deep cultivation in hard soil, but it can be guided just a ¼ inch below the ground level to stops weeds completely.

It may take a little practice to work this hoe to its fullest advantage, but with its' precise corners and some controlled handling, it becomes more of an instrument than a mere tool, in the yard or the garden.

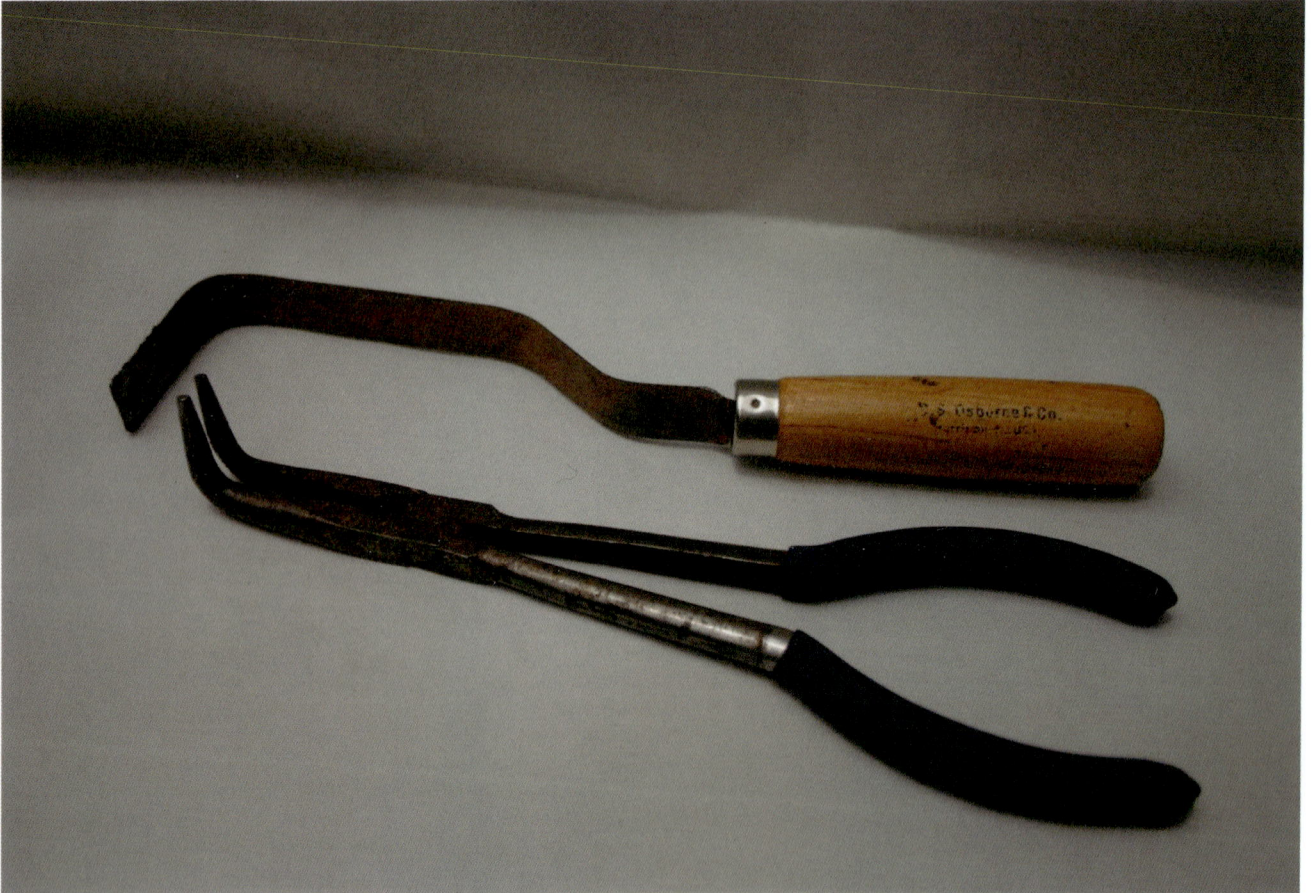

This next picture shows my two favorites for hand-to-hand combat. The weed hook is another tool that takes a little practice but can make a huge difference. Scraping over the surface to cut off weeds, or cutting deeper to cultivate with its' heftier metal. it gets the job done. The end allows you to trench, or start holes that can be developed with the body of the tool.

One outstanding capability of this tool is its' ability to help in pulling whole plants up out of the ground down to the finest roots. Using the hook you work under and around the clump, whether a piece of sod or a crabgrass plant or such, digging in hook first, but not cutting sideways around the plant. Loosen the soil, then grab the plant to keep tension on it and use the hook to pull up from underneath. With a little practice, you will feel where you have to shift the pulling hook, against the ground resistance, to pull the plant up whole, finest roots and all.

That may sound a little dramatic and self-indulgent, but how well this hook works is amazing. I found mine at a popular on-line store with a lawn and garden department. This hook is stamped with Osborne & Co., which might help you in finding a source.

The second tool above is a repurposed pair of long-handled right-angle needle nose pliers. I got the idea from using a small version for delicate gardening called a Japanese weeder. Same concept, just bigger and more forceful. The value of these comes from the ability to pull one weed or small plant at a time, going just below the ground surface to grab the root node. With steady straight pulling pressure, you will be able to pull the whole plant out, fine roots and all. I have a real problem with volunteer red bud and oaks and maples sprouting all over the yard and in my flowerbeds. Using this tool after a light rain, I can pull all 8 inches or more of sapling root out of the ground complete.

Reseeding

I don't think much needs to be said here beyond selecting a good seed for a good grass for your environment. I found my ideal seed by watching the groundskeepers at a local mall. I loved the turf, so when they started to reseed I asked them what they were using. If you can find what you like, ask the people who are succeeding. Do what works.

Having spent the earlier part of the year feeding the yard and eliminating the weeds, you should have a great canvas to work with. Cast seed might by itself might work fine. In more open patches you might want to work the soil VERY lightly, spread seed, and then tamp lightly to guard against it washing away. Think of the natural flow of things. The plants make seed. It falls to the soil. Nature works it in to germinate and grow. Your job is to lend a little assist for higher success rates. A forceful re-engineering of the process as you think it should work might be less than successful.

Selecting the grass you like for the area you live is too specific and complex for this short work, but I will say that some local advice and a little research on the prime temperature range and moisture for your grass of choice will go a long way towards a full, healthy lawn.

Remember, you are here to help Nature move in your direction. You are not going to succeed trying to bend it to your will.

Final Advice

While this presentation has been about lawns, and the weed pictures to follow are focused on lawn problems, don't forget about the perimeters. The edges of your yard and your flower beds can harbor weeds that are just waiting to get into the grass. Keep an eye on the edges. Don't encourage re-infestations by ignoring the flower beds. There are pre-emergent products specific to flower beds, if you don't want to use the lawn version. Mulch well. Don't let your guard down!

Identify the enemies!

The original intent for this book was to fill a void. I could not find any single place that had good pictures of the most common weeds that were making my lawn care life miserable. So this is it.

Following are picture identifications of the 32 weeds that I have found most common in my area. These weeds are found all across the United States, and probably elsewhere, so this should be a great aid for everyone fighting for the perfect lawn. There will be some on this list that might not grow in your area, and there will be some in your area that I don't have on my list. But these will should give you at least a solid 80%, and I would guess you are going to take out some of your other problems while dealing with these. The weed control tactics aren't so complex; they are widely applicable. This Rogues Gallery should get you a great start.

You will find the 'Treatment' for most of these weeds all the same: **Pre-emergent, post-emergent selective or non-selective, mechanical.** This is the sequence I would suggest; that is – prevent with pre-emergent, rather than fight after the fact. And, we are trying to enjoy our yards, so mechanical (i.e., weeding) is a last resort on a large scale.

Annual Bluegrass Burnout

DESCRIPTION: As mentioned above, this is not a picture of Annual Bluegrass, but rather the aftermath. Good pictures of the bright green clumps of pretty grass can be found on line. The problem arises when the Annual Poa starts producing seeds a couple of weeks after sprouting, leaving seeds for the Fall, and then dying out after preventing the good grass from developing.

TREATMENT: Pre-emergent, post-emergent selective or non-selective, mechanical.

Beefstake Plant

DESCRIPTION: The Beefstake plant was introduced as an herb and as a decorative, but in 7c and elsewhere it is invasive. It looks like a tall purple coleus and is very appealing – the first year. After that it is too late to have anticipated the thousands of seeds it generates and germinates. Above, you can see it starting to choke out my columbine. The plants can grow close together and have large leaves that block out sun and rain for anything below.

These plants have flower/seed tufts like coleus. Once you see these forming, it may be too late to kill off. Treat the areas with pre-emergent and keep an eye out next year.

TREATMENT: Pre-emergent, post-emergent selective or non-selective, mechanical.

Carolina Geranium

DESCRIPTION: Like a number of these weeds' Carolina Geranium is easily controlled in the lawn itself, but it takes refuge in flowerbeds for seed drift and grow out attacks. This is fairly easy to pull, but persistent and ever-present if it isn't controlled.

TREATMENT: Pre-emergent, post-emergent selective or non-selective, mechanical.

Carpetweed

DESCRIPTION: This plant can spread flat along the ground, bunch up a little as above, or grow up into mini-hedge formation about 6 inches tall. It usually will spread in a widening flower 'star' on an ever-increasing network of stems. As with Spotted Spurge, the larger plant will have one larger root base, so find that to pull by hand. Chemical control will work well, but repeated spot applications will be necessary. As usual, flowerbeds are its refuge.

TREATMENT: Pre-emergent, post-emergent selective or non-selective, mechanical.

Chamberbitter

DESCRIPTION: Chamberbitter is known by many names, though Mini-Mimosa probably comes in second. And it does look like a cute little mimosa tree. But... Seed production is prolific and comes within two - three weeks oof sprouting. These can be easily pulled in moist soil, but so many are germinated, you have to keep pulling and pulling and pulling.... Pre-emergent is the best way to get ahead of Chamberbitter in the flowerbeds. Normal mowing on a weekly basis will trim the tops and prevent seed production in the lawn.

TREATMENT: Pre-emergent, post-emergent selective or non-selective, mechanical.

Common Dandelion

DESCRIPTION: Everyone knows dandelions, and most lawn people dislike them as much as crabgrass. As can be seen above, the base of the plant forms a thick cover that disallows the germination and growth of the good stuff, so you have holes in the lawn once the mature plant dies. The good news is that with so many enemies, the dandelion is the target of many pre-emergent and selective post-emergent treatments as can be easily controlled. Mechanical control of some strays should finish the job.

Now you just need to get your neighbor to control his dandelions and the ever-blowing seedheads!

TREATMENT: Pre-emergent, post-emergent selective or non-selective, mechanical.

Common Vetch

DESCRIPTION: Above you see some Common Vetch getting started in the Liriope (Monkey Grass). The delicate twisting fronds can be attractive, and the delicate little purple pea-type flowers can add to the charm. The problems arise as the plant matures and spreads everywhere, choking some plants and generally causing a disorganized mess. Another culprit who hides in the flowers and perimeters and sneaks into the lawn. Lawn control is easy; flowerbed control is perpetual.

TREATMENT: Pre-emergent, post-emergent selective (with CAUTION), mechanical. I've taken non-selective post-emergent from this list and added a CAUTION to selective because Common Vetch has a tendency to find a home with ornamentals. Pre-emergent and mechanical are probably your best bets.

Crabgrass

DESCRIPTION: Crabgrass has developed such a reputation most weed control producers have some variant of control. Treated, it can be controlled, but expect recurrence and the need for repeated treatment. Left over roots, blown seed and birds are all working against you, but you can win.

TREATMENT: Pre-emergent, post-emergent selective or non-selective, mechanical.

Cudweed

DESCRIPTION: Like a number of these weeds' Cudweed can be easily controlled in the lawn itself, but it takes refuge in flowerbeds. Cudweed will be persistent and ever-present if it isn't controlled.

TREATMENT: Pre-emergent, post-emergent selective or non-selective, mechanical.

Dallisgrass

DESCRIPTION: A perennial weed, this can be one of the more difficult-to-control weeds. Dallisgrass has a leaf similar to crabgrass, but it is greener and shinier and grows more upright. In the lawn it stands out because of the lighter color and because it tends to grow a little faster, presenting tufts in the lawn.

TREATMENT: Pre-emergent, post-emergent selective or non-selective, mechanical. Dallisgrass can be persistent, so a non-selective should be used as soon as you find this one. It will spread quickly if not treated. This is one of those cases where a little collateral damage to good grass is preferable to too delicate a treatment that allows the Dallisgrass to spread.

Dayflower

DESCRIPTION: Not altogether ugly, but it is not grass. These leaves are about one inch long. You can see some of the thick stem in the top center of this photograph. Control can be difficult because of deep, intricate root system which regenerates easily. The proper herbicide and perseverance are the two keys to beating this one.

TREATMENT: Pre-emergent, post-emergent selective or non-selective, mechanical.

Dog Fennel

DESCRIPTION: Dog Fennel is distinguished by its singular stalk and its very fine leaf system. The plant can mature from 6 inches to 3+ feet. It is a perennial, so combinations of mowing and targeted post-emergent are the keys. This is rare in the lawn itself, but will readily crop up in flowerbeds and pots.

TREATMENT: Pre-emergent, post-emergent selective or non-selective, mechanical.

Dollarweed

DESCRIPTION: Another perennial weed. Note the round saucer shaped leaves on stalks. These leaves are smooth edged, but variants have scalloped leaves. If you haven't solved the problem, you will see little white flowers during the summer.

TREATMENT: Pre-emergent, post-emergent selective or non-selective, mechanical.

False (Cat's Ear) Dandelion

DESCRIPTION: This is not completely different looking than the Common Dandelion, except the flower appears on a tall, wiry stem, easily 12+ inches off the ground. In the picture above, I cut the flower down and laid it on the plant to get it all in focus. Notice how the leaf base of the plant creates an area where nothing else, good grass or weed, has a chance to grow. Then, when it dies out, you are left with a clump of rotting leaves and a hole in the lawn.

TREATMENT: Pre-emergent, post-emergent selective or non-selective, mechanical.

Goosegrass

DESCRIPTION: This is similar to crabgrass, except that the root is only at the center of the plant; it does not establish satellite roots. Chemical control isn't as successful as with other weeds and crabgrass, but environment is important. Goosegrass likes compacted high-traffic soil, excessive water and lots of sun. So- aerate as needed, guard against excessive water buildup and standing, and mow tall to eliminate or limit the availability of direct sun. I see this mostly on roadsides and the area around our neighborhood pool, which is high traffic and too close cut.

TREATMENT: Pre-emergent, post-emergent selective or non-selective, mechanical.

Horseweed

DESCRIPTION: Like Goosegrass, environment is important. Horseweed likes compacted soil and lots of sun. Aerate as needed and mow tall to eliminate or limit the availability of direct sun. I see this mostly on roadsides, but flowerbeds and (as above) flower pots can also be called home.

TREATMENT: Pre-emergent, post-emergent selective or non-selective, mechanical.

Nutsedge

DESCRIPTION: Nutsedge grows from a single root base and matures to tubers quickly. With its dainty little seed pods and dark clean blade and stem structure, I find the individual plants somewhat attractive, but I prefer to admire them in someone else's lawn. These plants and their seeds can be so abundant and widespread that mechanical control is not reasonable. Because of the tuber plant base, post-emergent control id probably the most logical answer, and that will need to be applied repeatedly and the weeds reappear.

TREATMENT: Pre-emergent, post-emergent selective or non-selective, mechanical.

Pigweed

DESCRIPTION: Notice the full leaves just left of center. This is the initial state for pigweed (clustered here in the middle of yellow oxalis), but insects love the stuff so you will often see the chewed over mess pictured above.

This plant will succumb to good lawn control (mowing tall, neutral pH, watering, thick grass) but it can find refuge on perimeters and flowerbeds and thus maintain a constant presence. Even plants that have been cropped can mature if left alone. I have seen reports of over 130,000 seeds being produced per plant! Treat as noted, and remain vigilant.

TREATMENT: Pre-emergent, post-emergent selective or non-selective, mechanical.

Plantain

DESCRIPTION: Again- large leaves blocking out the growth of anything else, good or bad. Easily controlled if treated. Otherwise you can have spots or whole swaths of bare ground to wash away once the plantains die. Notice that only a few Spotted Spurge plants have made any headway into this patch, and that, in itself, is not a good thing anyway.

TREATMENT: Pre-emergent, post-emergent selective or non-selective, mechanical.

Poison Ivy

DESCRIPTION: Three-leaf clusters are the identifier for tis nuisance. Sometimes you see waxy shiny leaves, sometimes matte. Sometimes more serrate leaves, sometimes smooth. This is a fresh sprout from seed, but it is common to find it vining across the ground or growing up and enveloping trees. Here it is trying to protect the Stiltgrass to the right.

TREATMENT: Non-selective post-emergent, mechanical. Everyone knows about poison ivy, so deal with this by pulling as your own sensitivity allows. In 7c, I find this in shoots spread all over the yard, from seed. Try to avoid burning this. I have known people who were so sensitive they developed blisters inside their lungs from breathing the smoke.

Smartweed

DESCRIPTION: The largest of these leaves are only 2 inches long, so this is not overly obtrusive, but it grows fast and finds refuge in flowerbeds where it is safe from the post-emergent. Most lawn problems can be easily solved and result from seed drift and out-growth from the flowerbeds. One of the big marks against Smartweed is that deer love it. If you want to deer standing on your lawn, that may be a good thing. But those same deer standing on the lawn eating your flowers and shrubs tends to create an attitude shift.

TREATMENT: Pre-emergent, post-emergent selective or non-selective, mechanical.

Spotted Spurge

DESCRIPTION: A pest. Notice the little dark spots in the center of the leaves. Another flowerbed regular that finds its way into the grass. Controllable in the lawn, persistent among the flowers. Spotted Spurge and the cat keep coming back. Just a pest.

TREATMENT: Pre-emergent, post-emergent selective or non-selective, mechanical.

Stiltgrass plant

DESCRIPTION: You will see evidence of Stiltgrass in the wild in many of the other photos, such as on page 50. Notice the long boat-shaped leaves mixed in with the White Clover. The horizontal line on the paper above represents ground level, so you can see the 'stilts' supporting the main vine. Manual weeding results in broken little pieces of vine and root left behind, which regrows rapidly. Once started, it spreads in a quickly widening patch, either choking out grass and other weeds or creating a mat around the bases of plants. As mentioned in the text of this book, showing any mercy to Stiltgrass means you have just lost.

TREATMENT: Pre-emergent, post-emergent non-selective, mechanical. Hope the pre-emergent works, otherwise non-selective post-emergent is the only reasonable solution. Expect collateral damage to good lawn; you must be thorough. Get the plants when you first see them; if they go to seed you will have another year of problems.

Thorny Olive

DESCRIPTION: These glossy, innocent looking little fellows can be the beginning of big problems. The Thorny Olive grows prolifically, new shoots on established plants easily growing 6 0 feet in two months. Great for highway dividers, it grows out to 20 by 20 foot hedges that stops headlights and runaway cars. But the branches look like vines and grow in every direction, making it nearly impossible to groom. It has one week a year of glorious scent, which only temporarily mesmerizes you into ignoring the 52 weeks of evergreen, thorny, branching, ugly confusion.

TREATMENT: Pre-emergent, post-emergent non-selective, mechanical. This is invasive in 7c, spreading by seed and far-running roots. If you find any, you can probably count on pulling saplings for the rest of your lawn care days. It is like playing whack-a-mole with green things.

Virginia Copperleaf

DESCRIPTION: These plants are a few inches tall, but this will grow to a lanky foot. Like Smartweed (and often found together) this is easily controlled in the lawn itself, but it takes refuge in flowerbeds for seed drift and grow out attacks. Fairly easy to pull, but persistent and ever-present if it isn't controlled.

TREATMENT: Pre-emergent, post-emergent selective or non-selective, mechanical.

White Clover

DESCRIPTION: This certainly looks better in a field from a distance. The dull green of the well-known three-part clover leaf with dusty white patches and the straggly flower tufts are not going to win any beauty contests up close. This grows in patches, so it chokes out most other things trying to grow amongst it. Notice the pointy boat leaves of the nearby Stiltgrass that can't even penetrate the heart of this clover patch.

TREATMENT: Pre-emergent, post-emergent selective or non-selective, mechanical.

Wild Carrot

DESCRIPTION: No carrots. Instead of the 'bunch' of greens you would expect from carrots, this plant has a stem that can grow up 12 – 18 inches. Usually singular plants popping up on their own, these plants can be mowed down to die off in the lawn, but if they are in the perimeter they will be back.

Not a serious offender, but the picture above is about as attractive as it gets. It doesn't age well.

TREATMENT: Pre-emergent, post-emergent selective or non-selective, mechanical.

Wild Strawberry

DESCRIPTION: Also called Mock Strawberry and Indian Strawberry, I believe those names came about from this plant mocking the lawn caretaker and as an aspersion against Indians. Another pest, the fruit is small and inedible, the flowers small and only fleetingly attractive, and the plant is relentless. In truth, post-emergent may be the best bet as the plant vines and deep roots as it goes. You will never pull all of the soft roots, if you can even find them all. This grows low to the ground with wide leaves, blocking the growth of desired grasses.

TREATMENT: Pre-emergent, post-emergent selective or non-selective, mechanical.

Wild Violet

DESCRIPTION: Looks like a violet. Hard-to-get-it-all rhizome type root. Develops little violet flowers, but not controllable enough or pretty enough to gain favor. Note how the bunch of leaves blocks the growth of good stuff.

TREATMENT: Pre-emergent, post-emergent selective or non-selective, mechanical. This is a prime candidate for repeated spot treatments of post-emergent as it has a tendency to One of the biggest difficulties in eradicating this weed is its' appeal to some members of the household with its "cute little violet flowers."

Yellow Oxalis (Wood Sorrel)

DESCRIPTION: This cloverleaf weed also comes in a purple-brown version. Little yellow of violet flowers. It doesn't look bad for about 2 days, and then gets long and straggly and spreads all over the place. This can also develop to plants 12 – 18" tall. (Notice the Spotted Spurge to the bottom right.)

TREATMENT: Pre-emergent, post-emergent selective or non-selective, mechanical.

CONCLUSION

This book is a result of wanting to share what I have learned from my years of playing "Is it weed? or is it wonderful?" I hope a few lawn care strategies and a set of pictures to single out the greatest offenders will help you focus your efforts and make your lawn care and yard care a lot easier and more efficient.

Make a schedule and stick to it. Give yourself two full seasons to get well ahead of the curve. And know you can't stop. All it should take is the weed and feed and some spot treatments and you will have years of lush lawn to enjoy. But remember- birds, wild animals, the wind and your neighbor's weeds are all waiting for you to let your guard. Stay in the game!

Good Luck & Good Fun!

22725675R00033

Printed in Great Britain
by Amazon